An Introduction to American Antique Glassware

By

Alice Van Leer Carrick

Copyright © 2011 Read Books Ltd.
This book is copyright and may not be
reproduced or copied in any way without
the express permission of the publisher in writing

British Library Cataloguing-in-Publication Data
A catalogue record for this book is available from
the British Library

OLD GLASSWARE

IF, Gentle Readers, you should learn later that I am languishing in a county jail, you must understand that it is all your fault. You see, I was ambitious; I wanted to know everything that could be known about the charming old glassware that you pick up now and again at sales and shops and auctions and little out-of-the-way places. And such information is expensive; a body can have but an academic knowledge of what she has never bought. I need n't, I am sure, go on with my sad story. As yet I have n't expended any vast sums, but my feet are firmly planted on the downward path, for old glass has always had what I am tempted to call a holy fascination for me. I do not know anything more engaging than these delicate things that have lived so long — so fragile, yet so resisting time; nor yet anything so eloquent of hospitality; and, if I am being ruined, it is in a high cause.

The illustrations and my words, I hope, may convert you, also, to this divine madness, but better still and more certain would be examining the old pieces themselves, handling them, if you may, for if you can get the "feel" of the texture, you are on the way to becoming a discriminating collector. Indeed, one connoisseur I know tells me that there is no more final way of testing old glass and china than by touching it to the tongue — somewhat after the fashion of the old-time laundress who "tasted" her irons to see if they were the right temperature. I have tried this honestly and with my eyes shut, but I cannot yet tell the tongue-difference between a Lowestoft cup and a modern piece of similar size and texture. I merely give it to you for what it is worth.

There isn't much use in my trying to write the history of glassware in one short chapter, is there? If you don't agree with me, a casual stroll through the glass-rooms of the Metropolitan Museum will convince you, I am sure. You all know that the art is as old as time itself, that it came down from the early Egyptian days, and that the Phœnician legend may be even a truth. In the Museum there are several pieces of Sidonian glass, and one cup, a dull amber-green, bears an inscription which, translated, runs, "Let the buyer remember."

Ah, far-away, dead-and-gone buyer in that distant time and town! Truly, "the bust outlasts the throne, the coin Tiberius." And the Romans used glass, so we are told by one authority, much more commonly than we do now, — read Machen's "Hill of Dreams," and see how beautifully he paints its color and loveliness, — and, where they colonized, there their glass was also made. Even in Great Britain there are traces of Roman glass-making, and the fires of the

Collection of Mrs. Carleton.

Early nineteenth-century glass picked up in northern New England. The cruet and decanter are especially interesting.

Enameled Stiegel mug, flower and pheasant design — an unusually fine specimen in "proof" condition.

Collection of Shreve, Crump and Low Company.

Waterford glass, late eighteenth century — unusually fine and stately pieces, beautifully cut.

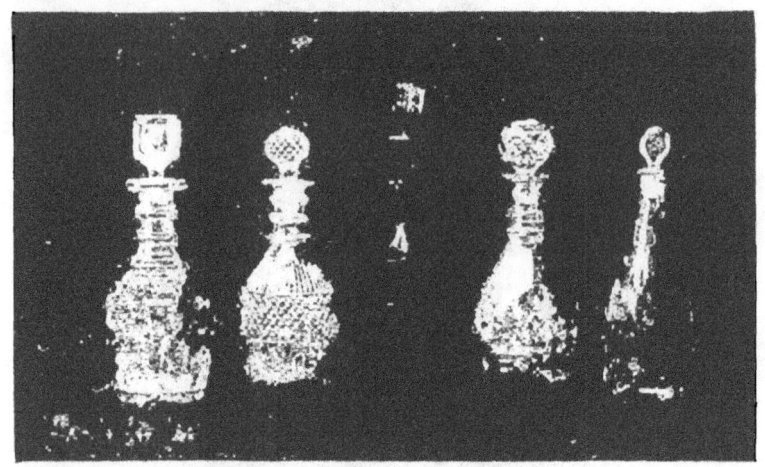

Collection of Dr. Coburn.

Five decanters, each one of a pair, two cut, one Bohemian, one pressed, one blown. Notice the difference in the decoration and in the varied stopper shapes.

craft died down and burned up through the centuries, until they reached a steady flame of excellence in the late sixteen-hundreds. You have heard of the glory that was Venice and the grandeur that was Bohemia; but, as I am quite sure that none of us are going to discover Portland vases or authentic Verzellini wine-glasses, I am just telling you the short and simple annals of the various pieces I chose to point my moral and adorn my collecting-tale. For many of these quaint and charming pieces were picked up here and there through the New England countryside, and the first group, as you might guess, is L——'s. It is a pity that you cannot see more clearly the attractive etched festoons that adorn the decanter, the wine-glasses, and the little cruet. The tumbler — L—— has a pair of them — flares slightly at the top, and is decorated only with a ring of ridges, and probably all five pieces are early nineteenth century. L—— owns also the beautiful Stiegel mug. The enameled decorations, pheasant and flower, naïve in their coloring, sturdy tones of green, blue, yellow, and red, are perfectly preserved, and as clear as they were the day they came from the glass-works of "Baron" Stiegel.

What an interesting human being he was; what an individual personality he has written into the pages of America's manufacturing history! Some day you must read Mr. Hunter's delightful study of this man and all his works, for I can give you just the barest details. Heinrich Wilhelm Stiegel was born near Cologne on May 13, 1729, and, after his father's death, came to America with his mother and younger brother. His early struggles, his connection with the iron business, even then flourishing in Pennsylvania, his marriage to his master's daughter, his increasing prosperity, his magnificent style of living, and his real merit, have been admirably and accurately related by Mr. Hunter. So much legend surrounds the man! And perhaps he was not all that grandiloquent tradition testifies; but I am so glad that "The Feast of Roses" has been reëstablished at Mannheim, where he erected his first glasshouse, and created an artistic craft, in itself a feather in America's commercial cap. You see, once he cast his bread upon the waters by canceling the debt of the Lutheran church there, "one red rose annually in the month of June forever" to be the only payment, and now, on the second Sunday in June, roses are piled within the chancel-rails of the Zion Lutheran church at Mannheim, and a red rose is sent in fee to one of Baron Stiegel's descendants.

He brought the tradition of his craft from Germany where glass-making had been an art for centuries. I realized this when I saw at the Metropolitan Museum a little green glass pitcher with the applied thread design, found at Cologne and dating from the third century, for it has much the same feeling, color

Engraved and initialed white flint Stiegel tumbler, with a short baluster stem. The engraving is unusually good.

Both of these tumblers are from the Hunter collection in the Metropolitan Museum.

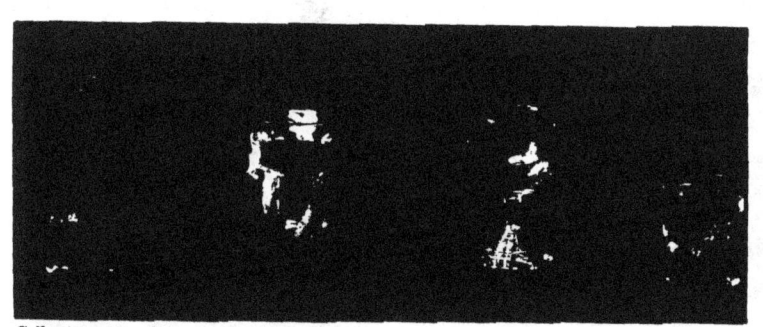

Collection of Dr. Coburn.

The first and third are Stiegel pieces, the other two the later type.

A Stiegel bottle from the Metropolitan Museum, known to have been done by Sebastian Wilmer, one of Baron Stiegel's imported workmen.

White flint toddy-glass from the Hunter collection, in the Metropolitan Museum. These glasses with tops are very rare.

Collection of Mrs. Carleton.

So-called Stiegel glass, but in reality made in the early nineteenth century. From the inscriptions on the mugs they may have been intended for children.

and "air" as some of Stiegel's own work made hundreds of years later.

He even imported workmen, — the lovely flowered bottle is the achievement of one of them, Sebastian Witmer, — but he was a most loyal American, and it is said that Elizabeth Furnace — one of his foundries and named for his first wife — was once the only place where Washington's army could get cannonballs. He protested vigorously against the importation of foreign goods, and it was a keen chagrin to him to feel that, to sell his wares in Boston and New York, the dealers had to assure their customers that they came from across the water. Baron Stiegel's rise was rapid; his fall even swifter; his success, while it lasted, phenomenal; and the tragedy of it is that this American craftsman-genius should have died in utter poverty, and been buried in an unknown grave.

Stiegel died in 1785, but the feeling of this enameled glass that he introduced lasted on until the nineteenth century, and now and again you will find pieces of this type sold as Stiegel. But while they are thoroughly charming with their gay little colors, and certainly related, though distantly, they are not his work at all. The group of two tumblers flanked by the two taller mugs will show you precisely what I mean.

Of course, glass-making had been attempted early in the history of our colonization, the year 1607, in Jamestown, marking the first venture. It is said that

Italian workmen were brought over to assist in the enterprise. But no definitely good, artistic work was accomplished until the days of Wistar and Stiegel in the middle eighteenth century. Glass was imported from England and the continent as soon as the settlers had adjusted themselves to fairly secure and comfortable lives, and continued to be imported, as I said before, even when America had created a craft of her own. The magnificent group of cut-glass épergne, compotes, and sweetmeat dishes (on page 116) is old Waterford, and though they have just come over, they are precisely what our beauty-loving ancestors bought when they could afford them. For Waterford in Ireland was one of the glass-making centres: beautiful cutting, rather shallower than we moderns interpret cut-glass, was done there until the excise duties in 1825 killed the industry. And "Venice glasses," such as you see in the long rows, were constantly imported during those early days. I am wondering just which of these patterns is like the ones Samuel Sewall describes in his Diary. "July 18th, 1687, — Mr. Mather had two Venice glasses broken at our Meeting." Now, as not one of this godly company could be described as a "lewd, roistering fellow," I am attributing the destruction to the sweeping results of religious fervor.

Bristol was an important glass-centre, too, and the late-eighteenth-century decanters (on page 116) — almost the finest I have ever seen — and this

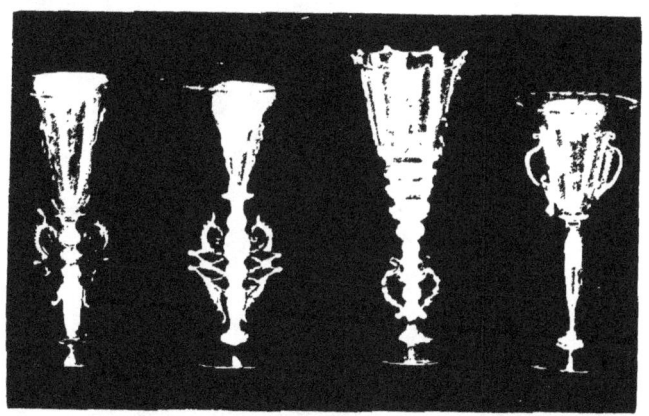

From the Metropolitan Museum.

Fragile Venetian glasses, delicately shaped and charming through their bubble-like transparency. Notice the elaborate stems.

Collection of Dr. Coburn.

Three opaque Bristol pieces quaintly decorated.

From the author's collection.

The "Lafayette decanters." Late eighteenth-century cut-glass pieces from Bristol, England, the pattern delightful and individual.

group of three milky, opaque glasses probably came straight from that city. There were three other decanters, and we call them the "Lafayette decanters" because, in 1824, — when he was being fêted all over America, — the set was sent down by my ancestors to be used at the big civic banquet given in Nashville, Tennessee, in his honor. These three descended to my side of the family; quite perfect they were, too, except for one tiny nick on the further one, and that happened when my grandmother kept open house during the Polk-Clay campaign. My mother just remembers it; she was a tiny thing then, dancing about the big old hospitable Southern yard, and the gay-colored lanterns, each representing a state, — a yellow one for "little Rhody," — hanging there in the dusk made an immense impression on her childish mind. As did, also, a big coon, for some reason a Clay mascot, running up and down and rattling his chain in the tall walnut tree. All this for the "Clay Guards," for my family were Old Line Whigs; and the next night everything was darkened as if for some tragedy when the "Polk Fusileers" paraded past the house. They still tell a story of their captain stopping at the gate to ask an old negro standing beside it why there were no lights, and what his master's politics were, whereupon the darkey answered, "I disremember, Sah, but I knows he is what you is n't!" Somehow, these decanters seem to me to hold memories as glowing as the wine that has filled them. Do you wonder that, in their later years, they are treated with the greatest care and consideration? And at Bristol they still make the opaque glass; I saw a piece the other day, more sophisticated, but I do not think possessing any more charm than these quaint scenes that resemble the mediæval, red-roofed Troy Town that Swinburne and Rossetti describe.

Bristol, too, stands sponsor for some of the charming eighteenth-century wine-glasses, of all things my desire, and what I am going to collect as soon as ever my ship comes a-sailing in. England, you know, had for some time been making glass successfully. A Venetian, one Jacob Verzellini, worked in Crutched Friars, under a patent that dated from 1575 and was to last for a quarter of a century. There are three of his glasses still to be seen: one at Windsor Castle, the other two in the British Museum, carefully preserved as very precious evidences of that early glass-making time. Later, the Duke of Buckingham, always interested in his country's manufactures, established a glass-furnace at Greenwich, and in 1673 Evelyn records in his Diary, "Thence to the Italian house at Greenwich, where glass was blown of a finer metal than that of Murano, at Venice"; and, twelve years later, he notes, "his Majesty's health being drunk in a flint-glass of a yard long."

And then from 1690 to 1810 — the dates are approximate only — these delightful wine-glasses were made: baluster-stem, plain-stem, air-twist, white-twist and cut. There they are, rather roughly classified, and the bowls are even more numerous: the Drawn, Bell, Waisted Bell, Straight-Sided, Rectangular, Ovoid, Ogee, Lipped Ogee, Double Ogee, and Waisted. When you have mastered these details, you may feel, as I did, very much as the White Queen must have felt when she had "believed as many as six impossible things before breakfast." I have given you such a list of names that I almost hesitate to describe the types of feet; but I will risk it, for there are only four principal ones: Plain, Folded, Domed, and Domed Folded. The fold was to give additional strength, the dome to make the glass sit evenly on the table and keep the roughness of the "pontil-mark" from scratching the wood. And, by the way, always remember this, that a glass with a pedigree has a "high instep," and if you find one very flat-footed, or, except on the cut-stems, with the "pontil-mark" ground away, the chances are that the glass is spurious. For fakers are beginning to copy these old wine-glasses very skilfully indeed, because the price that the genuine glass brings is temptingly high — so very high, really, that nation-wide prohibition assumes the aspect of a twofold blessing. But this for our comforting: even the cleverest copier in the world cannot reproduce the effect of that silvery air-twist, the twist that grew, perhaps by accident, out of the adorning "tear" in the stem, for the process has been lost, and we are safe in purchasing that type — if we have the money!

I have a theory which I hope you share. All of us, at least all of us with romantic tendencies, no matter what our political principles, are Jacobites at heart, are n't we? I know that you would have rejoiced with me in a very fine collection of Jacobite glasses that I have just seen: glasses that Harry Esmond, before he broke his sword and renounced his allegiance, might have drunk from as he toasted "The King over the water"; glasses engraved with the oak tree, thistle, and the Stuart rose with its two buds, emblematic of James the Second and the Old and Young Pretender; even with the portrait of "Bonnie Prince Charlie" himself. Others were inscribed with "Fiat" (the Cycle Club's motto), "Redeat" and "Audentior Ibo," each earnest of the hope that breathes in the old Scotch song "Better lo'ed ye canna be; will ye no come back again?" And would n't you like to own some of those dram-glasses (on page 130), fashioned of lead-glass, thick and heavy at the bottom? "Firing-glasses" they were called, because of the noise they made when the roisterers thump-thumped them on the table in applause. Would n't they make you see the long, smoke-filled room, the hospitable board, and, through the haze, Tom Jones and Humphrey Clinker and the beloved Uncle Toby sitting there?

Of course, all inscribed glasses are not Jacobite; I

Courtesy of Brooklyn Museum.

Jacobite glasses engraved with the oak tree, thistle, and the Stuart rose with its two buds, emblematic of James the Second and the Old and Young Pretender; even with a portrait of "Bonnie Prince Charlie" himself.

Courtesy of Brooklyn Museum.

"Firing-glasses," so called because of the noise made when the roisterers thump-thumped them on the table in applause.

am thinking of one — such a slender glass — in this same collection, engraved "Herte be true." The gift of some lover to his lass, maybe; but, just to show you that all sentiment was not confined to the mother-country, let me tell you of a pair of engraved flip-glasses, large ones, that live in one of Mr. Francis Bigelow's loveliest cabinets. The first is marked "John," the second "Mary." Now, who was it that defined domestic happiness as "two pairs of feet on the fender?" I constantly think of this happy Colonial couple, sitting together before a blazing hearth, with these glasses full of steaming flip, rocking and sipping in harmony.

Collecting old glass is such a joy! Once, in a little, shabby suburban shop, I found a charming decanter; early nineteenth century, cut a little, engraved a great deal — and I gave it away to one of the most attractive women I know, a friend who loves old glass quite as much as I do. And parting with it wasn't a pang, really, because my collecting creed tells me that you must never keep what you could not give away, nor give away anything that you would not willingly keep. Another "find" is the cut and engraved cruet (on page 133), which might be either Spanish or Dutch, for both countries so reacted on each other. It is one of the finest pieces of glass I ever saw, and D—— and I bought it for a song — an expensive song! You could buy several Caruso records for what we paid — in a little, dark downstairs shop on an ancient side-street that used to be one of the "green lanes of North Boston."

And those big, browny-olive bottles with their rough pontil-mark at the bottom can so often be picked up at country auctions. One such time is as indelibly engraved on my memory as the designs on those old glasses I have been showing you. My first auction it was, too, and I think I have never seen so many desirable things all together at once at any other country sale: a Hepplewhite secretary, slat-back chairs, copper-lustre pitchers, a Nanking coffee-pot, — I got that! — a little, squat, jolly brown "Toby," — the only piece of Bennington I ever wanted, — and this lovable, old, fat, green bottle. We were terribly excited, R—— being especially agitated. He had motored miles to get that Bennington "Toby," and he meant to have it. The desire of his whole collector's soul shone eloquently in his eyes. The bottle was put up for sale first, and he bought that. Then, clasping it in his arms, he sat awaiting the Bennington treasure — and near a Franklin stove! Here is the crux of the tragedy; here, perhaps, you discern the beginning of the end. Up and up went the bidding, and, finally, as R—— stretched out trembling, triumphant hands to seize his trophy, he knocked the bottle against the edge of the stove, and crash, smash, like the "Luck of Edenhall," went all that old greeny glass in fragments at his feet! So, you see, you must remember when

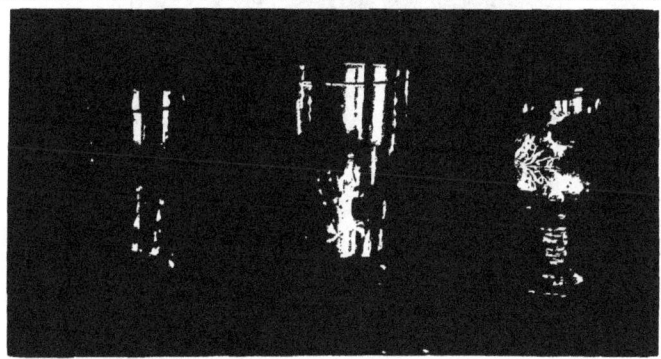

Collection of Francis Bigelow.

An interesting group, two flip glasses and a celery holder, all beautifully engraved.

Collection of Mrs. Carr.

Cut and engraved Spanish or Dutch cruet. A very fine and dignified piece standing twelve inches high. The sides are slightly flattened and beautifully decorated.

Courtesy of Metropolitan Museum.

These quaint old browny green bottles have charming decorative qualities.

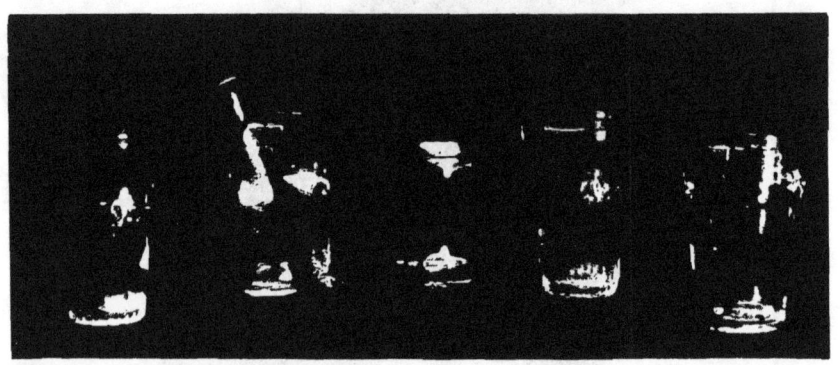

Collection of Dr. Coburn.

Five flip glasses, each also one of a pair. The second with its toddy stick is very interesting.

you buy one of these ancient bottles to be very careful. Remember, too, that they are delightful receptacles for certain flowers, the hardy, homely sort: roses are too delicate, but pink phlox, pink snapdragon, and, above all, pink peonies, become their naïve, simple quality admirably.

When I was a small, wondering girl I used to stop, caught by the rainbow beauty of the iridescent Cypress glass in the Museum, and dream over this loveliness that had outlasted the ages. Now I know that my youthful enthusiasm meant that I should live one of the most ardent protestants to be of all charming antique glassware.

CPSIA information can be obtained
at www.ICGtesting.com
Printed in the USA
BVHW032005110721
611678BV00006B/236

9 781447 444565